MATHEMATICS CRACKER

A COMPLETE REFERENCE OF MATHEMATICS FOR CLASS 8TH

RAMEEZ AHMAD

Made with ♥ on the Notion Press Platform
www.notionpress.com

Contents

Preface

This book is written in the hopes of sharing the excitement found in the study of mathematics. Math can help us unlock the mysteries of our universe, but beyond that, conquering it can be personally satisfying. We developed this digital book with the goal of helping people achieve that feeling of accomplishment.

This book is compiled and designed from different sources in order to remove the Mathematics phobia among the students. Most of the students use guide in mathematics which will only give them solutions. Conceptual knowledge plays a vital role in mathematics. This book contains three parts of every chapter. The first part consists of basic concepts about the Chapter, the second part consists of Solutions of all the questions with proper methods and the third part consists of multiple choice questions for revision.

Acknowledgements

COMPILED AND DESIGNED BY
RAMEEZ AHMAD
B.Sc (Non Medical), B.ed
M.A Economics

CHAPTER ONE

RATIONAL NUMBERS

NATURAL NUMBERS

Natural numbers are set of numbers starting from 1 counting up to infinity. The set of natural numbers is denoted as 'N'.

WHOLE NUMBERS

Whole numbers are set of numbers starting from 0 and going up to infinity. So basically they are natural numbers with the zero added to the set. The set of whole numbers is denoted as 'W'

INTEGERS

In simple terms Integers are natural numbers and their negatives. The set of Integers is denoted as 'Z' or 'I'

RATIONAL NUMBERS

A rational number is a number that can be represented as a fraction of two integers in the form of p/q, where q must be non-zero. The set of rational numbers is denoted as Q.

For example: −5/7 is a rational number where -5 and 7 are integers. Even 2 is a rational number since it can be written as 2/1 where 2 and 1 are integers.

STANDARD FORM OF RATIONAL NUMBERS

The standard form of a rational number can be defined if it's no common factors aside from one between the dividend and divisor and therefore the divisor is positive.

PROPERTIES OF RATIONAL NUMBERS

CLOSURE PROPERTY OF RATIONAL NUMBERS

For any two rational numbers a and b, $a*b=c\in Q$ i.e. For two rational numbers say a and b the results of addition, subtraction and multiplication operations gives a rational number.

Since the sum of two numbers ends up being a rational number, we can say that the closure property applies to rational numbers in the case of addition.

The difference between two rational numbers result in a rational number. Therefore, the closure property applies for rational numbers in the case of subtraction.

The multiplication of two rational numbers results in a rational number. Therefore we can say that the closure property applies to rational numbers in the case of multiplication as well.

In the case with division of two rational numbers, we see that for a rational number a, a÷0 is not defined. Hence we can say that the closure property does not apply for rational numbers in the case of division.

COMMUTATIVE PROPERTY OF RATIONAL NUMBERS

For any two rational numbers a and b, a∗b=b∗a. i.e., Commutative property is one where in the result of an equation must remain the same despite the change in the order of operands.

Given two rational numbers a and b, (a+b) is always going to be equal to (b+a). Therefore addition is commutative for ratoional numbers.

Considering the difference between two rational numbers a and b, (a−b) is never the same as (b−a). Therefore subtraction is notcommutative for rational numbers.

When we consider the product of two rational numbers a and b, (a×b) is the same as (b×a). Therefore multiplication is commutative for rational numbers.

Considering the division of two numbers a and b, (a÷b) is different from (b÷a). Therefore division is not commutative for rational numbers.

ASSOCIATIVE PROPERTY OF RATIONAL NUMBERS

For any three rational numbers a,b and c, (a b) c=a (b c).

i.e., Associative property is one where the result of an equation must remain the same despite a change in the order of operators.

Given three rational numbers a,b and c, it can be said that : (a+b)+c = a+(b+c). Therefore addition is associative.

(a−b)−c ≠ a−(b−c). Therefore we can say that subtraction is notassociative

(a×b)×c=a×(b×c). Therefore multiplication is associative.

(a÷b)÷c≠(a÷b)÷c. Therefore division is not associative.

DISTRIBUTIVE PROPERTY OF RATIONAL NUMBERS

Given three rational numbers a,b and c,

the distributivity of multiplication over addition and subtraction is respectively given as : a(b+c)=ab+ac and a(b−c)=ab−ac

NEGATIVES AND RECIPROCALS

NEGATION OF A NUMBER

For a rational number , a/b + 0 = a/b. i.e., when zero is added to any rational number the result is the same rational number. Here '0' is known as additive identity for rational numbers.

If (a/b)+(−a/b)=(−a/b)+(a/b)=0, then it can be said that the additive inverse or negative of a rational number a/b is −a/b. Also −a/b is the additive inverse or negative of a/b.

RECIPROCAL OF A NUMBER

For any rational number a/b, a/b×1=a/b. i.e., When any rational numbers is multiplied by '1' ,the result is same rational number. Therefore '1' is called multiplicative identity for rational numbers. If a/b×c/d=1, then it can be said that the c/d is reciprocal or the multiplicative inverse of a rational number a/b. Also a/b is reciprocal or the multiplicative inverse of a rational number c/d For example : The reciprocal of 2/3 is 3/2 as 2/3×3/2=1

REPRESENTING ON A NUMBER LINE

REPRESENTATION OF RATIONAL NUMBERS ON THE NUMBER LINE

In order to represent a given rational number an, where a and n are integers, on the number line :

Step 1: Divide the distance between two consecutive integers into 'n' parts.

Step 2: Label the rational numbers till the range includes the number you need to mark.

Similar steps can be followed for negative rational numbers by repeating the steps towards negative direction.

RATIONAL NUMBERS BETWEEN TWO RATIONAL NUMBERS

The number of rational numbers between any two given rational numbers aren't definite, unlike that of whole numbers and natural numbers.

There are "n" numbers of rational numbers between two rational numbers. The rational numbers between two rational numbers can be found easily using two different methods. Now, let us have a look at the two different methods.

Method 1:

Find out the equivalent fraction for the given rational numbers and find out the rational numbers in between them. Those numbers should be the required rational numbers.

Method 2:

Find out the mean value for the two given rational numbers. The mean value should be the required rational number. In order to find more rational numbers, repeat the same process with the old and the newly obtained rational numbers.

EXERCISE 1.1 :

Q1 :

Using appropriate properties find:

(

i)

(

ii

)

Sol:

(i)

(ii)

(By commutativity)

Q2:

Write the additive inverse of each of the following:

(i) 2/8

Sol: Additive inverse = -2/8

(ii) -5/9

Sol: Additive inverse = 5/9

(iii) -6/-5

Sol: Since -6/-5 = 6/5

Additive inverse = 6/5

(iv) 2/-9

Sol: Additive inverse = 2/9

(v) 19/-6

Sol: Additive inverse = 19/6

Q3:

Verify that - (- x) = x for.

(i) x = 11/15
Sol:

The additive inverse of *--x= x 1*

Put *x=1115 in equation 1, we get*

--1115=1115

⇒1115=1115

LHS = RHS
Hence verified
(ii) x = -13/17
Sol:

The additive inverse of *--x= x 1*

Put *x=-1317 in equation 1, we get*

---1317=-1317

⇒-1317=-1317

LHS = RHS
Hence verified
Q4:
Find the multiplicative inverse of the following.
(i) -13
Multiplicative inverse = 1/-13
(ii) -13/19
Multiplicative inverse = 19/-13
(iii) 1/5
Multiplicative inverse = 5
(iv) -5/8 × -3/7
Since : - 5/8 × -3/7 =15/56
Multiplication inverse = 56/15
Q5:
Name the property under multiplication used in each of the following:
(i) -4/5 × 1 = 1 × -4/5 = -4/5
Sol: 1 is the multiplicative identity.
(ii) -13/7 × -2/7 = -2/7 × -13/7
Sol: Commutativity
(iii) -19/29 × 29/19 = 1
Sol: Multiplicative inverse
Q6:
Multiply 6/13 by the reciprocal of-7/16.
Sol:

Q7:
Tell what property allows you to compute1/3× (6×4/3) as (1/3× 6) ×4/3.
Sol: Associativity
Q8:
Is 8/9 the multiplicative inverse of-1 1/8 ? Why or why not?
Sol:
If it is the multiplicative inverse, then the product should be 1.
However, here, the product is not 1 as

Q9:

Is 0.3 the multiplicative inverse of *313* ?why or why not?

Sol: *313=103*
= 0.3 × 10/3 = 3/10 × 10/3 = 1

Here, the product is 1. Hence, 0.3 is the multiplicative inverse of *313*
Q10 :
Write:
(i) The rational number that does not have a reciprocal.
(ii) The rational numbers that are equal to their reciprocals.
(iii) The rational number that is equal to its negative.
Sol:
(i) 0 is a rational number but its reciprocal is not defined.
(ii) 1 and -1 are the rational numbers that are equal to their reciprocals.
(iii) 0 is the rational number that is equal to its negative.
Q11:
Fill in the blanks.

i. Zero has ___________ reciprocal.
ii. The numbers ___________ and ___________ are their own reciprocals
iii. (iii) The reciprocal of - 5 is ___________.
iv. Reciprocal of 1/x, where x ≠ 0,is ___________.
v. The product of two rational numbers is always a ___________.
vi. The reciprocal of a positive rational number is ___________.

Answers :

i. No
ii. 1, - 1
iii. -1/5
iv. x
v. Rational number
vi. Positive rational number

EXERCISE 1.2

Q1:

Represent these numbers on the number line.

(i) 7/4 (ii) -5/6

Sol:

(

i)

can be represented on the number line as follows.

(

ii)

can be represented on the number line as follows.

Q2:

Represent *-211 , -511 , -911* on the number line.

Sol:

can be represented on the number line as follows.

Q3:

Write five rational numbers which are smaller than 2.

Sol:

2 can be represented as

147

Therefore, five rational numbers smaller than 2 are

Q4:

Find ten rational numbers between

-25 and12.

Sol:

-25 a��d12 can be represented as *-820 and1020.*

Hence ten rational numbers between *-820and1020 are-720, -620, -520, -420, -320,-220, -120,020,120,220*

Q5:

Find five rational numbers between

(i) 23 and45

Sol:

23 and45 can be represented as 3045 and3645 respectively.

Therefore, five rational numbers between are 3145,3245,3345,3445,3545.

ii-32 and53

-32 and53 can be represented as *-96 and106*

Therefore, five rational numbers between *-96 and106* are *-86, -76, -66, -56, -46*

iii14 and12

14 and12 can be represented as *832 and1632*
Therefore, five rational

numbers between *832 and1632 are932,1032,1132,1232,1332*

Q6:
Write five rational numbers greater than - 2.
Sol:

- 2 can be represented as *-147.*
Therefore, five rational numbers greater than - 2 are

Q7:

Find ten rational numbers between *35 and34.*

Sol: *35 and34* can be represented by *4880 and6080*
Hence ten rational numbers between *4880 and6080 are 4960,5060,5160,5260,5360,5460,5560,5660,5760,*

MULTIPLE CHOICE QUESTIONS
1. Rational numbers are closed under:
A. Addition
B. Multiplication
C. Subtraction
D. All the above.

2. The sum of *13,34 and56* is:

A.1223

B.2312

C.1512
D. 1

3. What is the value of *103 −14?*

A.94

B.912

C.3112

D.3712

4. What is the product of *12 and38* ?

A.316

B.416

C.516

D.616

5. What is the value of *-57 −23* ?

A. *-1021*

B. *-721*

C. *-1921*

D. *-2921*

6. *23 +57* is equal to *57 +23* .
A. True
B. False

7. Find the product of -73 × (54 ×29) .

A. *-1436*

B. *-3512*

C. *-3554*

D. *-5435*

8. (38 +27 +19) × *0* = ?

A.68

B.67

C.69

D. 0

9. What is the reciprocal of *727* ?

A.277

B. -277

C. -727

D. None of the above

10. *-1610* is not a rational number between -2 and 0.

A. True

B. False

ANSWER KEY

1. D
2. B
3. D
4. A
5. A
6. A
7. C
8. D
9. A
10. B

******************************END OF THE CHAPTER******************************

www.ingramcontent.com/pod-product-compliance
Ingram Content Group UK Ltd.
Pitfield, Milton Keynes, MK11 3LW, UK
UKHW061705190726
13853UKWH00008B/2417